CONSCIOUS TONGUES

Elenia Graf is a lesbian writer with autism. She grew up in Germany and now lives in the North of England where she graduated with an MA in Creative Writing from The University of Manchester in 2020. She was born with glass bones and paper skin, a fragile scaffolding for heavy words.

ISBN: 978-1-917617-07-9

Cover designed by Aaron Kent

Edited and Typeset by Aaron Kent

Broken Sleep Books Ltd
PO BOX 102
Llandysul
SA44 9BG

CONTENTS

Conscious Tongues

Elenia Graf

Broken Sleep Books

AUTOPSY

Who is the deceased?

i tried to think of myself as something other than hunger

Age:

i tried to think of myself as something other than just young enough
to be this hungry
i tried to think of myself as grateful
that i possess the anatomy required to eat

Sex:

i tried to think of myself as something beyond
my anatomy and remained in thought for a long time

Address:

before i performed an autopsy on myself i performed
an autopsy on the world
the world wasn't dead yet i had to kill it before
i sliced it open
inside i found suet
fleshy bodies unquestioned
and all the questioning bodies warped and beautiful
so there i went, inside the stiff world
and stitched its bloody underbelly
up from the inside

Length:

this is not an autopsy of my anatomy
this is an autopsy of my hunger

it goes very far

Weight:

it is very heavy

Eyes:

it is always growling
the loudest
when i can't see you

Hair:

it is always growing

Marks and Wounds:

the poet reports no visible bruises
or lacerations
you haven't touched me in a while
and you never touch me hard   enough

I. FEET

MY BUTCHER

before i ever held your hand
or watched you walk towards me
i wrote a poem for your boots

there is something to be said
for why dykes love
practicality and leather so much

i suppose worshipping you
goes hand in hand with histories
of codes and clandestine erotics

imagine us in the mid-century:
complicated courting schemes
of chivalry and coy rejections

i would have fucked the etiquette
and thrown myself at you
in the middle of a dingy bar

what i'm trying to say is
if i was a cow i would beg
to be sent to the abattoir

skin inside skin i'd carry you
my hide molded
to the arches of your feet

HOLY BATHROOM

___ shit stain ___ cistern! ___ trail of curls from door to bowl!
___ charcoal toothpaste painting the sink ___ drool
around your mouth like a rabid pup!
___ nail clippers tweezers pads! ___ foot scrubber
the butchest thing in this bathroom!
___ door, open. ___ shower ___ liminal space between fucking
and sleeping! ___ tap, towel,
water. ___ water. ___ water. ___ water. ___
___ drain pube ___ mystery puddle! ___ things under unholy
light emitting diodes!
___ brushes ___ devotees to the gospel of hygiene!
we foam and spit and rinse. ___ molars,
___ canine impulses, licking each other clean.

I USED TO DREAM ABOUT HOW IT WOULD FEEL

during the slow-rot beginning of the era after fantasy,
i learned how nausea is made:

poetically speaking, the sympathetic nervous system
redirects blood flow from the stomach to skeletal muscles.

sick friction writhes up the gastrointestinal tract like swallowing
a maggot in reverse. physically speaking,

i can't quite put my finger on why i asked him to rub my clit
after he raped me.

i like to imagine i was taking control of the situation. the dawn
of a new age in which i was touchable

and, above all, won at being hurt by choosing not to feel it.
i've done the maths

and my small intestine is approximately the length of two adults
lying down flat in a row.

i wish he'd only ever touched me foot soles to scalp. i wish
the stench didn't follow me

into every lover's bedroom as if my vomit is already in their mouth
before i had a chance to kiss it.

once molted, the skin of a snake is twice as long as the snake
that shed it. there is more

after loss. i come onto her hand and collapse into carcass. yes,
there is more:

necrotic want, bile, decomposed dreamscapes of intimacy. i try to count
the amount of it all. the absolute volume.

II. LEGS

after robbie spends / endless minutes pumping / into me / while i
pretend / i didn't say no first / i bury myself under / the duvet / of
my single / bed / robbie back at his girlfriend's / two weeks later
i suck / on his friend's cock / an even exchange for weed / though
i told him earlier / 'i'm not gonna / fuck you' / & by heterosexual
standards / i didn't / its fine / really / except i still cry when
i tell my therapist / about rhys / the blood / he left on my door
handle / & desire / a broken / word for teenage alcoholic / for
feeling untouchable / that is / unable to be touched / for fulfilment
/ of diagnostic criteria / impulsive behaviour / tick / chaotic
interpersonal relationships / tick / desire / from latin / *desiderare*
/ meaning to demand / or to long for / & aren't those / two very
different things /

    when her thigh presses / into me / i die / but in the way
a field / dies / in summer / the heat sucking / all water / out of
capillaries / green blades turning / golden / the white sky's /
breathy vacuum / all that was pumping / through the soil & the
stems / & the tiny veins emerging from the dirt / a body / of
steam hovering / above the rolling / blanket landscape / a kind
/ of summer no meteorologist / can explain / a kind of new that
rearranges / molecules in curious ways / solids / liquids / gaseous
words / you can choose them to mean what you long for / this is
what i hear / when she whispers / this is what i whisper back: / i
have been swallowing / wet earth / i am full / & turned / towards
the sun

SUMMER CAMP

marisa punches me in the face   when i don't stop singing
       football songs on the hike
my first and only fist fight   a one-strike affair
       that ends with my blood in ryegrass
that summer in '06   she chases boys around tents   blurry
       children in *bayern* jerseys
all of them sore we lost the world cup   in spite of the hymns
       and the camaraderie   i don't care for sports
i only sing the songs   for an arm around my shoulder
       like we're on the same team
marisa goes swimming with the boys   chucks her shirt
       in the sun-scorched field
by the river where the ground is humming   and from afar
       they look the same
cicada legs in sopping trunks   identical chests   children
       in high summer   one with a ponytail
us girls talk of course   about her curiosity
       that i am so curious about
that summer in '06   i learn that one can ask too many questions
       about another girl
when julia says it's weird   all the things i want to know
       about what marisa's like   if she wants to be something
and what that something is
each misarranged sentence   a placeholder   for words
       i haven't learned yet
i dyke child   stuck in that week in august   for another decade
       too much river water in my mouth   to unstrange strangeness
thinking the blood   the blood is what happens

III. GROIN

DIS-ASSEMBLY INSTRUCTIONS

think of something heavy, now drop
it to deduce the length of the descent.
we are in the place where it lands,
sweating.

\\

imagine the moon without craters.
imagine the sound that rang
everywhere
when it was engrailed.

\\

now imagine two hundred
and nineteen
moons, all falling
in the alley behind my house.

\\

hear the impact.
one by one cracking concrete. a breath
in my ear,
natural satellite.

\\

lift your head. watch them
cascading from this side of the window.

\\

fuck me through an avalanche
of moons.
and later, when we go outside
so i can smoke a cigarette,

we'll put them back
up in the night sky.
tiptoeing
with arms above our heads.

NESTING

i want to live under the buckle of ur belt / build a bed / beneath
the leather and denim / shape the wiry hairs into a nest / with my
saliva / my desires aren't strange: / some bird species do it / this
way / i can make it pretty / like i want to be / for u / i don't want my
hunger / to be rough / tangled twigs and bristles / i will decorate /
my hiding-place / with lavender and daisies / braided through the
growth / and i will never be too much / cuz there can never be /
too many pretty things / lover u know i bite / but only cuz i want /
to be bitten harder

at second thought / i don't think the flowers / could survive me
/ i can't be trusted / around beautiful things / they always find
their way between / my rotten teeth / can i still live / under ur belt
though? / can i still / cover u / with my spit? / lover u know / i
need a lot / it's my fault / for never feeling loved / unless i'm getting
fucked / i promise / i won't devour you / i'm baby swallow / i'm
naked hatchling / i will gobble / whatever you place on my tongue

IV. STOMACH

MEAL PLAN

i text you about all my meals so you know what's inside of me
when it's not you. these days i rejoice in cutting up beautiful
things other than myself. red onion, courgette, yellow pepper,
and too many cloves of garlic. when i miss you i send you the
mushroom emoji. when i want your attention i post raunchy pics
of myself eating raspberries on the internet. fragile fruit. i want to
store the way i feel when i'm with you in an empty jam jar. spread
it on toast each morning to get me through the doubt. i'd tell you
im havin toast for brekky. you wouldn't need to know the specifics
of what i use to appease my hunger. heather jam. i wouldn't even
be mad if the seeds got stuck in my teeth, i'd wave at everyone
and say *look i'm carrying bliss in my mouth* with the toothiest grin.
i'm trying to think of a time i've been satisfied for longer than
fifteen minutes. i'm trying not to make you the sole provider of
my satisfaction and succeeding. i cook sun-dried tomato soup.
buy a mango just because. when we met i stopped getting high
so i could stop lying about getting high. i'm trying to omit less
information. i have a list as long as the train track from your house
to mine. every bullet point a question boiling down to do you
want what's inside of me when it's not you

PIGS CAN'T LOOK UP

But I could pick a pig up one night and raise it into the sky and tilt this pig ever so gentle. I can make sure this pigs eyes line up with the stars. Imagine seeing the stars 4the first time. I want 2b treated that kindly and see the stars for the first time.
  — @vincentdonofrio on twitter, april 20th 2019

i.

i love you for doing my washing up

so i don't go into a state of depression

over the state of my kitchen, which

both represents and is caused by the state

of the world, which i cannot bear

to think about, truthfully.

ii.

i walk home from the shops with spaghetti

and fag papers, longing to carry a pig.

i would wrap my arms around its meaty torso

show it the clouds passing above.

iii.

i will cook food for you as long as i have hands

if you promise to stand at the end

of the day, towel on your shoulder, soap

water on the floor, all my plates and vessels dripping.

iv.

one time i watched you line them up,
dry your hands, and lift me off the sofa
although im six inches taller than you.
we laughed like this, content
but for the precarity
and when i dropped we laughed some more

v.

deep belly, snorting
oink.

THE WRONG KIND OF HOMO
after sam sax

first speech therapist says my syllables spill into each other / like sunburnt belly speeding down waterslide / splitting against sizzling plastic / unspooled stomach / tongue surrendering something bad / slit spewing spit / second speech therapist suggests exercises / stretching muscle / softly placing it / studying my sick / straightjacketing my sound / sellotaping my snake / have to do it before secondary school / or i will never be sexy / successful / stainless / at eleven / my tongue stabilises / stops seasoning my expression / i boast standard spelling / squeeze skin into system / secure girlhood / satisfactory until suspected lesbian / dykes don't speak / even if we possess perfect esses / society of secrets / silent class / dissolving history / boys / i love you / & your celebration / your associations / your intertextual soliloquy / salivating impediment that makes for superior sucking / slant of the wrist / saluting each other's soggy lips / maybe i am the wrong kind of homo / to have a lisp

V. CHEST

PURPLE

i'm purple for it
i'm pebble-smooth spit-slick pink around
the bottleneck
i'm crawling on all fours to your formation
and baby the floors are so clean

my skin is soaking in the sink
the rest of me yielding like wind chimes
to the thing that moves me
listen this is my lungs fluttering
like halloween angel costume wings

(do you think) i'm good (could you
tell me that) i'm good
(the floors are clean)
this morning i plucked three stray hairs
from my right nipple and one from the left

i'm cerise
opaque plum i rub condensation
on the windows
and moan at the droplets like lilith
if lilith had no power

you don't tell me to get up
so i glide to bed sponged and laved
i'm good (i whisper) it's only water
on the floors
surely you must see how hard i tried

PINK

peel my skin off in one smooth layer & i'm so pink underneath no
hair follicles to be seen such a lovely colour a bit like the sunset
sometimes or the doll-sized cardboard boxes lining the toy aisle
or the inside of my pussy i half unwoman half innocent repeat
& repeat the undressing of my flesh the surface of my body is
the wound i can't stop touching you know i told him i wouldn't
fuck him so we sat on the bed for hours smoking weed you
know i told him i wouldn't fuck him i just wanted to see where
it would lead you know i told him i wouldn't fuck him walked
him to my student accommodation anyway & they always liked
that i have cuts on my arms means they're allowed to hurt me
until i'm bleeding from my asshole & isn't that being young o
to be fuckable finally a smooth pink thing you can leave your
fingerprints all over and the ridges in their skin all felt the same to
me one was ginger one wasn't one was irish & i'm so bad at telling
accents lying there in my h&m bodysuit he asked must i unwrap
you like a present & i reached between my legs & unhooked
myself

VI. HANDS

RITUALS

i trim my fingernails
before i sit down to write poetry
i believe in the effectiveness
of preparing for the making

FANTASY POEM

where is my madonna
my britneys kings celestial dykes
or random man who hits the spot like cher
did for my boys?

i hallelujah in the hallway
cheer my baby on. those corduroys
make me want to stay in
watch her work, hard!

out the door no one wants
to be celebrated by us.
iconless audience
vibrator at the back of the drawer.

she hums against my earlobe
sucks glow from fresnel.
the strobe finally decides if it wants
the world to see and

sometimes i still want to hear a song
so good i cum on the dance floor
want to share my secrets with my boys
not borrow theirs.

what fantasy can i walk into?
the echo of her bicep against my palm
after unwrapping it.
heavy in our minutiae

bright in our stageless room.

VII. THROAT

TWO TONGUES

i'm sorry for mutilating you.
did you find what you were looking for?

cartilage. eggshell. grimy bathwater -
this is why you vomit sudsy shards when lovesick.

and the fattest feeling i have ever seen.
is my terror legible?

it pulses in our small intestine like a colicky baby.
i'm sorry for starving you.

try to explain your hunger to me.
it goes like this: i am a mouth. i am empty unless i am being fed.

what about your teeth?
i pulled them out to stop my gluttony.

is that why it's hard to speak?

what about your tongue?
i had a lisp. our mother cut it off.

you were already hungry then. she never liked that i was born holey.
porous. pitted. nurture slipping through my perforations.

is there a thing in this world that could sate you?
pomegranate seeds and fig meat. every thought of me that's
crossed my baby's mind on my tongue like a thumb. to bake red
velvet cake in my form and watch her chew and lick the plate and
the mixing bowl and the icing knife. love.

she has to lick the plate?
and the whisk and the kitchen counter and the measuring jug.
then i might be full -

      when i've filled her.

YES/NO/MAYBE

vaginal fisting
sounds so violent
until i think about you

r small hands
soap-rough
and always holding mine.

we lie side by side:
my shipwreck ribcage
your humid breath.

i can't taste your shame
in any place
my tongue reaches.

let's perform CPR
on our waterlogged
insides.

mouth to mouth to
yes/no
/maybe

you need to press
on the spot
repeatedly

for the water
to accommodate speech.
i am shaping

my hands into a bowl,
you may cough
we may unswallow.

MISPHORIA

i possess keratin, pigment, as well as specific
mechanical attributes to paper:
foldability, rigidity, and impact
resistance. paper possesses
cellulose fibres and the memory of pressure
making it. i hold a blood clot webbed
between my index and thumb and watch it gasp
for meaning. the inside outside me

sinew, eyelash, a plague of pigeons going to war
over a slice of bread. if i had a beak
no one on this earth would have eyes.
the nausea of the world
around the body. two fishes gorging on each other's tail fins.

until then. look at me. a clump of hair
and all these stupid organs: performer, stagehand,
pink skin ticket stub. have you ever unstitched
a suit and found a theatre - i mean, have you ever
clawed at velvet curtains and found cardboard siding -
i mean, have you ever slit yourself open from gum
to oesophagus trying to swallow
fish scales - the outside inside me

VIII. SCALP

OBJECT PERMANENCE/BODY DISAPPEARANCE

you are washing my back
with your peculiar sponge
shaped like a brain. it scrapes

my skin like it tried to be gentle
but couldn't help the urge
to remove a couple layers.

i wash all my folds with bare
hands. yours are on my shoulder
somehow more liquid

than the chlorinated water.
i hate that you always
want to shower after sex

like the sweat isn't hard-
won. like i don't dry
in gold flakes on your chin.

i push my nose into the mattress
when you leave the room.
i search my thighs for blue

proof of your presence.
i suppose i need the crumbs
to remind me that the meal

was good. you rinse the grip
of my fingers from your hair.
i comb them through your strands.

I'LL MAKE GOD REAL JUST TO BLESS US

i don't know how they do it in church
but it would go something like a touch
to the forehead whisper *you* a touch
on the breastbone whisper *will* a touch
to the stomach whisper *be* yours whipped cream
white molasses mine the bare-
boned frame made for something
soft to lay upon whisper *safe* a shiver
of water that has been rain before
and before and before i was alive to make god real
on our quiet crowns whisper *together*

SYNOPSIS

we dip into the foam, strike our pose
ornate silver spoon, embryo, breaststroke
on the mattress.
some nights she has me flopping
like a bucket of fish
and i her abdomen reeling
like a spool of thread unwinding
from my tongue.
under lunar zenith, we lap
at the high tide receding.
truth is, most nights we sleep like eggs
simmering in warm water.
her belly kisses my tailbone
bow to wave. i still fear
i will never be as happy as i want to be.
yet down gorges, down rivers,
down tongues bent backwards
no one has been this deep inside of me.
not spume
not even breath.

ACKNOWLEDGEMENTS

Thank you to Aaron Kent and Broken Sleep Books for giving these poems a home. To the journals that have published earlier iterations of some of them: *The Remnant Archive*, *The Sock Drawer*, *The Mechanics' Institute Review*, *BRAG*, and *The Cardiff Review*. To those who have taught me about both craft and soul, namely John McAuliffe, Day Mattar, and Brendan Curtis. To everyone who has ever sat in workshop with me. To butch and femme lesbians. And most of all to Kieran, my best friend, Hev, my love, and Peggy, my little dog.

LAY OUT YOUR UNREST